THE UNIVERSAL LAWS OF LEARNING

A Message of Hope

By

Tracy L. Brooker

THE UNIVERSAL LAWS OF LEARNING...A

MESSAGE OF HOPE

Copyright © Tracy Brooker and Associates, LLC.

All rights reserved. No part of this book may be used or reproduced in any manner whatsoever without the written permission of the author.

ISBN

Printed in the United States.

This is dedicated to my family

and all who have prayed for an answer.

Introduction

The American educational system is failing. From Sandy Hook to Columbine, and now teachers are "packing heat". America is clearly in a state of an educational emergency. Every school district has anti-bullying programs and the federal government is trying to nationalize a "one size fits all" curriculum known as the Common Core. Teachers teach for high achievement scores on standardized tests in order to receive funding and children are bored to death. So many teachers, administrators and parents are fed up. The end result is a boatload of children who are becoming numb to life. Even though it seems that the never ending educational black hole is unstoppable, well, believe it or not it can all change for the good. Yes, I said GOOD. Good for our children and good for the collective future that will someday reside on this place called Earth.

For many years now, people have prayed for an answer. They have prayed to change the chaos in our schools for peace and well-being. The irony is that the answers have been literally in front of us and within the same spiritual principles we choose to follow every day. The problem though, through our own programming and unconsciousness, we continue to submit ourselves and our children to the old paradigm of how education, learning and schools should be. By simply altering our thinking and becoming more conscious, our idea of learning and education can begin to be seen for the truth and power it has always held. As we begin to focus on what we truly desire, we open ourselves up to the greatness that lies within each of us.

As you read about the Universal Laws, allow yourself to think beyond schools and education. Take the time to think about yourself and your own educational experience. Go deep within yourself so to look for those programs you have believed about yourself such as worthiness. You may realize that there are many ideas that have stopped you from doing what you truly desire. This book is not just about our children, it is really about us and how our own awareness can help change and create the world we were truly meant to live in.

Growing up in inner city Cleveland I attended private Catholic schools. While attending high school and considering college my parents discouraged me from pursuing a degree in education. My dad felt the income would not be enough to become self-sufficient. He felt very strongly that I search for an occupation where I could support myself. My two sisters were already working in the medical field, so I followed their lead.

I ended up working full-time as a respiratory therapist then went back to school for my Special Education degree. After ending a divorce from an unconscious marriage, I moved to start a new life in Arizona. I headed west and quickly found a job in a small classroom. Later, I met my husband and birthed two wonderful boys.

I worked on and off in various settings when the boys were little: from special-needs preschool, resource, assistive technology, teacher trainer, deaf education, bottom line…I covered it all. Then everything changed. My oldest boy showed that he was having difficulties in school. My youngest became ill.

The elder son started to show signs of ADD, lack of curiosity and the basic boredom for school. He would come home crying because he would notice his papers wouldn't have smiley faces like the other children. The very school where I taught special education was calling me in for parent meetings on assessments, accommodations (such as longer time on classwork or needing frequent breaks to focus) and learning goals for him. And yes, there was a time where we placed our son on focus medications. (I am not proud of that time, trust me.) After one week, we took him off the medication. My gut kept telling me it was not the way. The day we stopped the medications, his very words were, "Oh thank you Mommy." That was a sign from the God within my son telling us what was best for him.

I never said I was perfect, let alone conscious. I did the best I knew at the time and I tell you that, if we had not gone through all of these challenges with our sons, I am not sure I would be writing this book. Everything does happen for a reason, and because of my experiences (and inexperience), I relate to my students, parents, and clients who struggle everyday with special education, compulsory education and the conditioned beliefs that children are taught.

Soon, we decided to homeschool. The boys and I would work on basic curriculum such as reading, writing and math. We all became bored quickly and decided to take homeschooling outdoors doing whatever we were inspired to do. I wanted our children to experience what life had to offer, rather than to read it in books. Once we gave up curriculum, our lives changed for the better. Whatever the boys wanted to do, we would do it, from video games (yes, I said the "V" word) to theater and improv. There was more time spent in the car rather than at home. Whatever sparked their interests became my job to find an experience where they would become immersed. Since we began what some call "self-directed" learning or "unschooling", we have been happier and more fulfilled.

With homeschooling and running an educational consulting business, I relied on and was vigilant with doing my spiritual practices. Between the struggles of caring for my youngest with chronic illness, and my oldest with a learning disability, it was my connection to Spirit that pulled me through.

My mother, grandmother, and great grandmother were all psychics and healers. From a very early age I would be able to connect telepathically to others. I knew how to consciously create things using thoughts and feelings, but unfortunately lacked understanding the consequences which came with those gifts. From energy medicine to connecting to lost loved ones, I have had many spiritual experiences. Spirituality is and always has been a vital part of my life.

The information in this book is a knowing that has been with me for as long as I can remember. My purpose is to share it with you, who are willing to confirm what you already know or to help you with whatever your struggles are with school, learning, or parenting. Whether you are a child, parent, artist or CEO, this information lies within each and every one of us waiting to be revealed, waiting to be recognized and utilized for our evolution and the evolution of Mother Earth.

This book will discuss the long time misunderstandings of what learning is. What you read may bring up feelings or questions, memories or nightmares of past school experiences or what your child may be experiencing now. Most important, whatever you are going through know that it is not your fault! Conditioning and compulsory education have been around since the fall of consciousness. In fact, many spiritual teachers have also fallen into the same ideals because they are simply so close to them. Spiritual teachers offer where and what kind of school to send your child. Their goals are to get us to become more conscious, more aware, but unfortunately they do not understand the significant roles that compulsory education plays and the repetitive conditioning it creates. This book is an extension of the awareness of what learning is and how free learning can help restore us, our children and our planet to our original pristine powers.

My intention is to deliver messages from Spirit's wisdom in order to provide caregivers of children an alternative, an AWAKENED alternative so as to transform what has no longer served us and our planet. My goal is to help any willing human who is searching to rekindle their souls with play, magic, and love. Perhaps it is your time to create what you truly desire.

I hope you enjoy this book and share it with many. The more people understand how to allow, raise, communicate and simply "BE" with children, the sooner this world can shift fully into Christ Consciousness.

Blessings!

Conditioning and Programming

Before the Universal Laws are defined, it would be helpful to define and discuss compulsory education. Compulsory education is exactly what states…compulsory. It is education that is coerced and enforced utilizing conditioned responses. Operant conditioning is a process of changing behavior by rewarding or punishing a subject each time an action is performed until the person associates the action with pleasure or distress. Conditioning utilizes both positive and negative behaviors, such as corporal punishment, grading, stickers and report cards. Whether in religion, politics or schools, compulsory education (and its conditional responses) has affected all of us in some way, resulting in a failing educational system, a failing economy and a failing environment. Compulsory education is a creation which stems from the unconsciousness mind.

However, as more and more individuals increase their awareness and consciousness, more opportunities can be created to change our existing stifled circumstances. How can that happen? First we have to take a closer look into today's educational myths and conditions which we have probably bought into.

You have to go to school to learn.

In the 1800's, an individual named Horace Mann brought the first public education model from Prussia to America. This system was strictly created from the booming Industrial Revolution in order to increase workers which resulted in increased profits. Prior to this, children worked at home, running farms, learning trades and eventually taking care of their own aging families. If a family was financially capable, children might have been sent off to a private school and then to college. When compulsory education first arrived to America, teachers were trained how to "educate" in such a way so as to produce an industrial society. In early educational history, "schooling" first originated from various religions that brought children (mainly boys) into synagogues and churches to learn their teachings and beliefs. The premise was that if they taught the beliefs early on, they could increase their followers. In addition, the earlier they taught the children, the faster the children would "believe" that what was told to them was the truth. To this day the cycle has continued.

If we take a closer look at Webster's definition of education, it in no place states that one must go to *school*. It is defined as the "process of imparting knowledge". Now, the definition of learning is the "process of gaining knowledge". Webster does not state that the learner **must** take in that knowledge. Therefore, the choice is to either impart knowledge, or to gain it. *It is simply a choice.* Unfortunately, society has been so coerced into believing that an individual must go to school to gain knowledge. *But that is simply not the truth.* In fact, a recent study by

U.C. Davis showed that if an individual initiates learning through passion and curiosity, true and meaningful learning takes place.

Learning is a choice. Even though our brains are continually active while information has been taught doesn't mean information has been "learned". Learning becomes a personal choice called Free Will. Free Will reminds us that *Source* has provided us with the opportunity to choose our experiences. Free Will reminds us that we are always connected to that *One True Source. It* never leaves us. But what does this have to do with education? Everything!

Almost anyone can choose to remember something, but that does not mean that the information is meaningful to them. A person experiences value in any given moment, when desired or needed. A person does not necessarily obtain knowledge when its "imparted" towards them. When an individual is consciously connected to what is being taught, they bring in Free Will to choose it. They will take and perhaps impart this knowledge. There must be a conscious choice, a conscious connection to transform this knowledge into meaning and relevance.

Take a moment to look at your own experiences. How many concepts did you really learn in school until something happened or until you had an experience that was meaningful which you could relate to? How many times have you heard someone say that it did not "click" until later, until they had an experience where they could relate to the knowledge? That's because when the information was presented, it was not relevant or meaningful to them at the time. A conscious connection was not present in order for the information to become meaningful. We can live in a constant state of learning, based on our own choosing. Therefore, learning is choice. Learning is **FREE WILL.**

You are empty until filled.

One of my favorite educational theorists is Paulo Freire. He spent most of his life fighting his country's government in order to create equal educational opportunities for the poor. He focused on "critical consciousness" where teachers would learn and understand students' social and emotional environment so as to create learning opportunities that were meaningful and relevant to the students. He believed in following a child's natural state of curiosity and felt strongly that children's minds were not "banking systems" continually needing to be filled. He was aware that an educational system of authority was where oppression began, where control and manipulation took over.

Instead of the "banking system", when we look at the idea of conscious education, there is simply nothing to fill unless an individual *freely* asks or initiates interest for information or an experience. Humans are born in "the perfect image of God," physical manifestations of the Creator. We are all created **FULL**, in that we have access to all the information we seek. Masters such as Jesus, Buddha and Gandhi have poignantly demonstrated this through miracles and peaceful resolutions. Yet, due to oppressive education, we have conditioned to believe that only teachers, clergy, family and society can provide information. If you do not attend "school" you are "less than."

Freire was ahead of his time. He was able to get his country to create a better educational system for the poor, but unfortunately, teachers continued to "teach" and children continued to be conditioned to believing that they were "less than." In society in general, children *are* told to believe this same idea. Elders are to provide guidance and counseling while children are to be seen, not heard and taught. These beliefs are simply false. These beliefs are disrespectful and therefore have led this world to its current state of crisis.

Let's take this a bit further...

If we are created in the "perfect image of God," then the truth is that children are equal in the deepest sense to any adult. Some might even argue that children ARE wiser because they lack the countless years of conditioning, programming, and false ideals hammered into them. Look at the story of Jesus going into the temple when he was only twelve years old. The Bible states that the elders were amazed at His knowledge and understanding of Jewish law, without ever having stepped into the temple, the place where Jewish law was taught. How many times have we heard of children having memories of past lives or exhibiting natural intuition, gifts and talents beyond their years?

Simply put, children are perfect! In the Present moment, there is nothing to teach children. They are already full with whatever information they need. Their physical minds lack years of conditioning therefore, they have access to what is known as the ***Collective Consciousness*** and the vast knowledge It has to offer. The Collective Consciousness is the set of shared beliefs, ideas and moral attitudes which operate under the ***Unifying Force of the Christed Consciousness.*** We all come from, participate and have access to the Collective Consciousness. Unfortunately, through our own conditioned learned behaviors, we forgot our true nature and the unlimited possibilities that we can create through our connection with the Collective Consciousness.

God is Love. We are created from Love and when consciously connected to Source for the highest good of all, we are able to create that which is a blessing for all. We are also able to learn, absorb and allow ***Source*** to move through us guiding our next sacred experience.

When children are born, they arrive in perfect vessels for their Divine nature, without any conditioned habits. We acknowledge children as innocent and perfect, and once they begin to move or create sound, we begin to condition them by saying things such as, "No, don't touch that!" or " No, stop that!" or "Yes, do that again." These conditioned habits have been taught for generations. But if we let children explore without conditions, learning from their intrinsic natural curiosity and passion, they are able to access the Collective whenever they so choose because the conditioned habits are nonexistent. Accessing the Collective will allow them to evolve happily with the guidance of their higher selves.

The children who have had the good fortune to experience self-directed learning or 'unschooling" have higher success rates because they are supported in their learning based on their interest, desires and personal timing. Dr. Peter Gray, a well-known psychologist, conducted a study with adult" unschoolers", and found that these students showed a higher success rate in pursuing academic degrees based upon their interests, simply because they were not controlled or coerced under limiting environments. Their lack of experience within a traditional compulsory school system has allowed them to learn whatever they choose, driven by personal interests, curiosities, and passions. These, children and adults, are succeeding educationally, economically, and emotionally.

When the Soul is given freedom to explore and express *Itself*, without being coerced, conditioned or stifled, *It* has access to the **Collective Consciousness** to learn whatever *It* so chooses or desires, resulting in a state of joy and fulfillment. These students experience life as a conscious choice. They are not outsiders or victims of circumstance. Their focus is on being the **Conscious Creator** they came here to be, making choices based upon joy, fulfillment, and passion, rather than what they are forced to do. They can be the *Conscious Creators* they came here to be. Some of these children even choose traditional schooling after having the experience of *free* schooling, but it is of *their own* choosing, rather than that which is forced upon them. When they consciously choose to go to schools and universities they embrace and follow their personal intrinsic motivator to obtain a degree. That's where the difference lies! When school becomes a choice and not a forced activity based upon success and failure, school becomes a successful system rather than a failing one. The failing system IS exactly as what it created. Force, coercion and manipulation create an unhappy, stressed society. A school that embraces FREE WILL and unconditional learning creates what it graduates…an AWARE and CONSCIOUS society.

Universal Laws of Learning

Universal Laws are the steady and unchanging principles that govern the universe in order for the world and entire cosmos to continue to exist, thrive and expand. The Universal Laws of Learning in particular, govern how beings in physical form learn and create within a physical dimension such as Earth. These laws are extensions of the Universal Laws. They provide a framework as to how each soul can learn from the physical world and manifest whatever it is they truly desire.

A vital part of the Universal Laws of Learning is the understanding that each individual is what is known as a Creator God. Sorcerers, wizards, gnomes, fairies and angels, and yes each Soul has the innate potential to experience being a Creator God. Think about it…why are stories such as *Harry Potter, The Hobbit,* and *A Wrinkle in Time* become so popular? It's because deep within each Soul lies a memory and experience of True Magic. It's the

Magic every child dreams about, like on Christmas Day which is full of innocence, joy, playfulness and love. Similar to Harry Potter's wizardry, Merlin and the Fairy Godmother, each of us embody the very qualities and abilities to create magic in physical form.

The Universal Laws of Learning are *Divine Oneness, Curiosity, Imagination, Creation, Play, Nature and Grace.* Each chapter is designed to not only define each law, but it will also provide toolkits for those who are looking to reconnect with or to heal something within. Each Law has been divinely guided by Spirit in hopes to reawaken the Creator God within you, as well as to provide a spiritual blueprint in order to guide future souls who have incarnated to create a world full of Peace, Love and Harmony.

Divine Oneness

Divine Oneness is God's infinite wisdom that lies within each and every thing and being, always available, always within our reach. It is the "ah ha" moment, the "gut feeling", the "I was just thinking about you" minute. It is the inspired poem, song, or work of art and the complexity of surgeon saving a life. It is beauty, laughter, grace and the innocence of children. It is our connectedness to Source.

Divine Oneness is also the loss of a loved one, the tears of crying baby, or the breakup of a marriage. Divine Oneness is simply **God** experiencing ***Itself*** through us, emotionally, mentally, and physically. We are the sacred physical carrier, a ***Creator God*** and unique aspect of Love ***Itself*** in physical form, here to experience a physical dimension in evolution. Many of us asked to be here to experience the transition of Earth back into its perfected form. Part of the awaking, part of consciousness is to become aware not only of conditioned habits that affect our awareness, but most importantly to stop the stifling patterns that impair our future and our children here on Earth.

When the fall of consciousness occurred, humans became "separated" from their connection to the God within. Biblically it was called the "Original Sin". The animal and fairy kingdoms separated themselves from humans. This separation resulted in instinctual behavior within the animal kingdom and veils that separated humans from the Elemental and Fairy Kingdoms. Some animals remained to assist humans with memories of unconditional love, while others chose to stay in the wild. Some fairies have shown themselves to humans and they assist with nature, while others have remained in the "unseen."

If you watch a child you will see many of them talking to their imaginary friends. There is nothing imaginary. Because they have less conditioned habits, they are able to see Fairies and connect with animals on a much deeper level than many adults. They can see and feel their Angel's presence and the presence of those who have passed on. They can remember past lives and even connect with beings of dimensions unseen to the human eye. They are connected, without ego, living in the present moment experiencing whatever is arising within them.

Children live this way until an experience happens. This glorious way of living lasts until man, woman, school or religion tells them "NO". We tell them what to say and when to say it. We make them wrong because children are expected to act a certain way, look a certain way, or do what we tell them to do, supposedly all in their best interest. In our conditioned minds we try to control for better outcomes. And as we impart this conditioning, ego becomes reinforced and the connection to Source diminishes. But, if we allow children the space to connect to the Divine in their own way, through a natural state of curiosity and interests, then True magic happens.

Research

There has been substantial research supporting the effectiveness of intuition. In a recent study conducted by the University of New South Wales, researchers used a series of experiments to determine whether people were using their intuition to help guide their decision making process. (Nierenberg, C. 2016). They defined intuition as the" influence of nonconscious emotional information from the body or the brain," such as a gut feeling or sensation. The results showed the following:

- That when the participants were shown positive subliminal images, they performed better at guessing the answers.
- They were more accurate, responded more quickly, and reported feeling more confident in their choices of answers.
- The experiments also suggested that the participants became better at using their intuition over time.

- The study show that information subconsciously perceived in the brain helped with decision making as long as that information hold some value in their conscious mind.

The more we allow children to guide themselves utilizing their own intuition, the more they can make conscious decisions for their lives confidently and joyously.

Biblical Reference

In the story of Christmas, or Jesus' birth, the Savior arrives in physical form, saving the world from Original sin. The actual story provides so much more. Everyone knew that a "God" would be born unto the earth. Both Mary and Joseph prepared and accepted that their child would be the "Son of God". There was nothing to "teach" him. They were aware of His gifts and for obvious reasons did not have to "teach" Him. They showed us that if every parent brought their child into this world, feeling and thinking children were Gods, miracles would happen. Mary and Joseph showed us that trusting in our children could literally and ultimately save us and the planet.

In Isaiah 59:1-2, sin is defined as a "separation from God." If every child was seen as a Savior, then sin (separation from God) would cease to exist and the awareness of Source within would be experienced throughout us. Children are born present, "closest to God" because their egos have not had yet have had time to mature. If we remember, if we simply followed their lead in becoming more aware and conscious, then "sin" (separateness) simply falls away. That is why Jesus loved being around children. He was aware of their innocence, joy, and connection to Source. Just as Jesus, when we give children the space to be free, to be uninhibited by curriculum, testing and competition, to play and be creative, they show *us* the path to enlightenment, the path to connecting to the God within.

Many have written that when we are born into this duality dimension, we "forget" who we really are. This is only partially true. We become disconnected from the "feeling" from the *All That Is* consciousness. We still have awareness, but once we as children are exposed to the many conditioned environments, the veil (or as some say, the illusion) takes shape. That is why it is so important to be aware of ourselves, especially around children so as to not impose our conditioned habits onto them. They will have to navigate and endure this dimension on their own one day as it is. But creating a space for them to decipher what is meaningful to them helps them to come closer to their own soul, their own unique expression of Source.

Parents/Caregivers

Breathe, Pause and Observe. If there is anything you can take away from reading this book, the most important part would be to observe your children. They will tell you when they are tired, hungry, or in need safety or space. They may not articulate in adult terms, but they are always communicating to you their needs. There is nothing to teach for they are already full of knowledge from Source. By following your own intuition you will know when they need you and how to respond. If ever in doubt, simply ask them.

Most adults are conditioned. We have a tendency to fix, teach and do. Taking a moment to stop to see what is occurring without analyzing, fixing or teaching is a tremendous shift in your own spiritual evolution. Children require unconditional love. Love without conditions. They are Love, just as you are. They are not empty requiring you to constantly fill them up. Our job is to assist when needed, with basics such as food, water, protection and love. They will watch you and model after you. They will learn from the Universal Laws around them.

The best way to listen to your children is to observe them. See their actions without analyzing. Ask them how you can help during times of stress. Love them in silence, with gentle hugs, smiles, or a caring note. Remind them often that they are Gods and they have the ability to create anything they desire through Love. Thank them for their presence, and if they are too young to talk, say to them, "Creator God, what will you show me today?" Allow them to be your greatest teacher, and you student, always listening, always learning from them.

In 1968, two researchers, Rosenthal and Jacobsen showed that teacher expectations influence student performance. Positive expectations influence performance positively, and negative expectations influence performance negatively. (Pygmalion Effect, 1968) If you were to see, think, and believe your child is an extension of God, a Creator God, then the performance you will see will be as such. If every parent believed this one simple thought, imagine how the world would be. Imagine a world without destruction or suffering, imagine Heaven on Earth.

As adults we can continue to heal from our past and from the generations of conditioning which have been incarnated upon us. We can learn to meditate, to practice conscious awareness, to eat high vibration foods such as organic vegetables, and learn to silence our minds as much as possible in order to create a quiet space for our own connection with the Divine.

In as little as one simple breath, you can connect, for you are your own unique expression of God, a Creator God. By breathing in deep, dropping the diaphragm and pushing the belly out, then exhaling and bringing the belly in, you can ease the conditioned chatter. The benefits of meditation are priceless such as emotional peace and well-being. You can include in your meditations feelings of well-being sent to your base chakra and send love to your heart. Even while on the road you can apply these techniques of practicing well-being and love. You will begin to notice a shift in your perception and a shift in your awareness. The feelings of love and well-being are who you really are. They are your connection to Source. They are You.

Essential Oils, Crystals, Angels, and More

Frankincense and vanilla, either combined or separate, placed on the base chakra (at the bottom of your spine) and heart chakra will help with augmenting awareness and intuition. Amethyst and Angelite, either worn or placed near or in your space of meditation, increase the energies of intuition. Tanzanite can be used to connect with your Soul Star which is slightly above the head. Calling on Archangel Haniel can help develop your intuition and clairvoyance saying the following prayer. "Dear Haniel, thank you for helping me to connect with the Divine." Finally, by calling and focusing on the elementals of Light, they will provide light to darkness, glitter to water drops, and the rays to the sun, and will help in the connection to Source through warmth, light, and comfort.

Story of Divine Oneness

My father passed away when my sons were 3 and 5. I remember one day driving in our minivan. My 3 year old began to have a conversation with someone apparently sitting in the front seat (physically no one was there).

I heard, "Knock, knock." Then there was silence. My son said, "Orange." Then silence again. My son continued, "Orange you glad I didn't say banana?"

I turned and said, "Michael, who are you talking to?" He said, "Dziadek." (That's Polish for Grandpa.) I responded, "Where is he?" Michael pointed to the front seat and replied, "He's right there Mommy, can't you see him?" My response was, "I can now."

See, children have no filter. They can see angels, fairies, remember past lives, talk to animals, and yes, talk to those who have passed on. It is only our adult ego, our conditioned habits and beliefs that keep us from having those same experiences and memories. If your son or daughter sees or hears something from the "other side," do not belittle them or tell them it's their imagination. In fact, it is more real than the current reality you may inhabit. Let them show you the magical side of consciousness filled with love, joy and laughter.

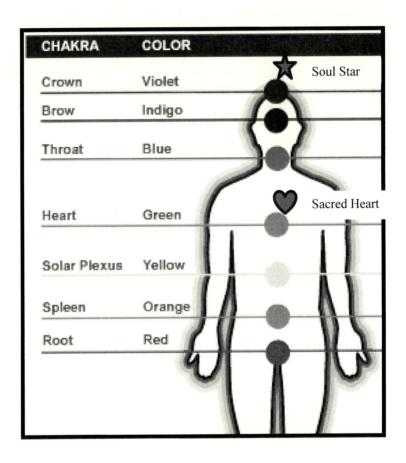

This diagram above shows the 7 chakras, their associated colors and areas on the physical body.

Examples of Self-directed Learning

Built a Treehouse

Teen Improv

School of Rock

The Butterfly Story

Homeschool Shakespeare Theater

Homeschool Fencing

3rd Movie Premier, Main Character

School of Rock

Junior Olympic Archery Division

Raising Chicks

Homeschool Skiing

Deep Sea Fishing

Curiosity

Curiosity is a spiritual sense that leads an individual to seek out information or an answer. It is Universal wisdom asking us to follow a lead or to move in a certain direction. It's a gentle nudge towards an individual's next sacred moment. When curiosity happens consciously, there is no judgement, no opinion but a pause for discovery. There is a sense of wonder, preparing an individual for the next thought, the next process or experience.

When we constantly tell children what to do and how to do something, we remove their natural sense of curiosity. Then the information they receive simply becomes rote, boring information. When a child follows a lead based upon natural curiosity, the energy created stems from their Higher Self providing them with the Free Will to choose their next holy experience.

Research

In October of 2014, U. C. Davis conducted brain research based upon curiosity. They originally performed the study to help individuals with neurological conditions. Their research showed the following:

- People were better at learning trivia information when they were highly curious about it.
- Curiosity was "like a vortex that sucks in what you are motivated to learn, and also everything around it."
- When curiosity is stimulated, "the part of the brain that was related to reward was greatly stimulated, and there was increased activity in the hippocampus, a brain region that is important for forming new memories, as well as increasing interactions between the hippocampus and the dopamine reward circuit."

- When curiosity is stimulated in the brain, the dopamine effect takes place.

The dopamine effect regulates movement and emotional responses, and enables an individual to see rewards and take action towards them. Dopamine increases attention, improves cognitive function, and stimulates creativity. It makes us more social and extroverted and helps us form romantic and parental bonds. It helps with sleep, mood, and the overall health and well-being.

When students are not given opportunities where curiosity drives learning, then the dopamine effect cannot take place and the overall feeling of well-being is non-existent. Creating learning opportunities where curiosity precedes learning provides optimal outcomes for the pleasure center to become stimulated, which in turn affects positive health and well-being of the child. Can you imagine a Universe that has provided all the physical capabilities that support mind, body, and spirit?

Biblical Reference

In John 4:48 Jesus said, "Unless you people see signs and wonders, you simply will not believe." The story is about how Jesus helped a royal official by healing his sick son who was close to death. Jesus asks us to keep a sense of wonder, as the unemotional observer in order for miracles to happen.

When life brings us down the human brain naturally wants to worry, fix and control situations. The brain has been trained to think and react in a programmed manner with generations of habitual conditioning. We come here and experience the duality dimension, the highs and lows, with everything in between. That is how *Creator* experiences *Itself,* through us. When we let our emotions override awareness, our human soul gets lost. When our brains becomes quiet and we let a sense or feeling of curiosity come through, the chatter of the mind slows down enough to help us proceed to the next step. Being curious keeps judgement and other analytical thoughts from ruining our experiences and allows Spirit to simply guide us.

People came to follow and see Jesus' work not because they knew that He could perform miracles. They heard about him and became curious. Their curiosity led them to learn more about the Son of God who could perform miracles. Their own curiosity led them to their personal and spiritual transformations. Jesus said, "Truly I tell you, unless you become like little children, you will never enter the kingdom of heaven." (Mathew 18:3) By having a sense of wonder and curiosity, you are able to become aware of your connection to Source. When we are connected to Source, possibilities are endless.

Parents/Caregivers

Wanting to guide or tell your child what to do seem obvious since we want nothing more for our children then to be safe and happy. We want them to make the right choices in hopes that they make it through each day unscathed. Often, children are being bombarded, whether through technology or from those around them which simply takes away the space where the joy of being curious can blossom. We tell them what, when, how, and why without even giving them a chance to figure it out on their own, even if they wanted to. Then when they are teens we are troubled because they don't want to communicate with us, or they rebel, when they simply are just "trying things out", coming into their own awareness and strength.

Taking a step back and becoming curious of our child's behavior is literally transformational. It creates a pause to facilitate listening on a level you never thought possible. When a teen is screaming will you hear through your heart?

"I'm struggling and I just need you to listen". There is nothing to do but to be there for them, unless they ask otherwise. If you feel yourself leaning in, wanting to fix or teach something, ask their permission to do so. If a child falls and cries, become curious, comfort them, without explaining what they did. They know they fell! Love your children with a sense of curiosity so that your relationships will blossom. You might notice that you will slowly lose the feeling of and perhaps habit of overreacting, finding greater peace and calmness. Once you practice curiosity and wonder in your own personal space, you may begin to see all the little miracles your family has to offer.

Through the many years of compulsory education and living within a conditioned environment, no wonder that so many in society feel like a bunch of clones that wake up, go to work, come home and repeat. It's the never ending hamster spinning a wheel. However, by simply learning how to become more aware of our thoughts to quiet the mind, and allowing some feelings of curiosity, we can change our perception of our daily experiences. If you suffer from writer's block, you might experience playing with the thought of being curious. If your boss yells at you, what might happen if you are curious? If your car won't start, can you be curious? Curiosity will create the pause before emotional reaction takes over. Start with a few seconds then extend it a little longer. The longer you are curious, the less time your mind has to chatter, worry or stress.

While in meditation, try focusing on the feelings of curiosity and wonder, feeling your energy become lighter. If thoughts arise, allowing them to simply move through you like a gentle breeze on your face helps in relaxing the mind. You can even try giggling a little, being curious about your thoughts. Focusing on joy and simply being happy, like a child on Christmas morning or a birthday.

Being curious about the energy of your Higher Self invites you to your next sacred moment.

Essential Oils, Crystals, Angels, and More

When you massage a small amount of the essential oil of Neroli, or orange citrus blossom on the forehead the oils can help restore the sensations of curiosity and wonder. The crystal citrine may impact you to create more curiosity when placed near or around your head. Calling upon the elementals of wind help to whisper in your natural curiosity and may provide a gentle whisper of pause and wonder. Finally, calling on Angel Zadkiel to help heal emotional chatter and enable more curiosity and wonder to your life by saying, "Dear Zadkiel, thank you for helping me to remember a childlike sense of wonder and curiosity."

Story

My oldest son came into this world with a natural sense of curiosity. He was so curious that for many hours he would keep a conversation going with my husband, asking questions about fishing, never letting up. My husband and I would laugh because while most children his age would fall asleep in the car during long trips, he would stay wide awake asking questions all the way home.

When he began struggling in school, I noticed his joy for learning and his natural curiosity diminishing. I remember that right before I offered him to homeschool, he asked me that if we were to do classwork, could he get smiley faces and stars on his papers like the other kids in his class. I reassured him he could put stars, smiley faces, whatever he wanted on his schoolwork because it wasn't about how he did, but about learning what he loved.

When we switched to self-directed learning, my son's love and curiosity has returned! Now that he is in community college, he is consciously aware of "playing the school game" in order to get his desired degree. He knows he has choices in teachers and some classes, and is willing to be patient to find those that keep his joy for learning intact. He still has a way to go before getting a degree in engineering, but he is willing to play the game in order to reach his goal. Whether alternative schooling or alternative ways of learning, he is willing to find whatever works in order to receive his degree. And as his parents, we will be there to support him, no matter what schooling looks like for him.

Imagination

Imagination is the female side of energy. It is the intuition and joyful innocence combined with the essence of Universal magic. Imagination flows into the building blocks or geometry of physical manifestations called *Creation*. It is circular in nature and flows down from the Higher Self and Soul Star into both the emotional and physical bodies.

Imagination holds imprints from past, present and future dimensions. Imagination flows together with free will in order to guide our choice in what we desire our creations to be. Most individuals are unaware of its uses but when conscious, they are able to connect, focus on their feelings and create what they want.

To children, imagination is part of living until it is erased or measured by the new conditioned environments they may experience. The so called imaginary friends are as real as the physical world, and children are able to see and communicate with the many beings such as Fairies, Angels and Elementals. The imaginary friends and other dimensional beings have purpose and information to share with children and us!

Research

Cognitive scientists hypothesized that our ability to imagine mental images and to create new ideas is the result of something called a "mental workplace." Dartmouth College took this information a little further by using MRI technology. They had participants look at images and then while under MRI, destruct, reimagine and reshape the images. What they found was that not everyone's responses derived from the same brain area. They saw that learning new concepts, and seeing things from different perspectives had a lot to do with a "very rich mental space, a kind of a mental playground." (Ferro, 2016) As far as imagination and creativity, the brain used multiple areas verses just one.

Sir Ken Robinson, who is an expert of learning and children's education states that "Imagination is the source of all human achievement." (FirstPlace, 2015). Learning to think outside the box and coming up with innovative ideas takes imagination. He defines imagination as "The ability to bring to mind things that are not present to our senses." He elaborates by describing imagination as "The primary gift of human consciousness. In imagination, we can step out of the here and now….revisit and review the past."(http://www.conversationagent.com,2015)

In 1968, George Land conducted a research study to test the creativity of 1,600 children ranging in ages from three-to-five years old. Sadly, he found out that the older children became the less creative and imaginative they were. He felt that creativity had been buried by rules and regulations, based upon an educational system designed to train good workers. (http://www.creativityatwork.com,2017) The more conditioning and training of the young brain, the less creative and imaginative they become.

Biblical Reference

"So God created Man in His own image, in the image of God He created him; male and female He created them." (Genesis 1:27) Because Man (a.k.a. human) was imagined and created in the image and likeness of God, so too can Man imagine and create all he desires. "I tell you, whoever believes in me will do the works I have been doing, and they will do even greater things than these…" (John 14:12) The disciples had asked Jesus to show them "the Father". Jesus explained to them that they have seen the Father, not only through Jesus being the "Father" in physical form, but through themselves as well as. Jesus reminded the disciples that God lived in all of us, and that Humans, when conscious and aware could and would perform greater works than He. When we connect with Christ consciousness, we are capable of performing miracles just as Jesus was able to. With the joyful, light attitude of a child, and the knowing that God works through us, anything we imagine can be created.

Parents/Caregivers

A child's imagination is more precious than gold. Adults hold on to the many conditioned habits that can block pure imagination from coming through. Because a child lacks the many years of conditioning, their imagination has less of the illusionary veil and can therefore, when focused, able to create from a space of purity and power. There is no judgement, no reason; there is only pure uninhibited excitement while exploring the world around them.

If your child has imaginary friends, try not shaming or dismissing them. Welcome them and ask your child to share if they want to tell you about their special friend. Consider it a blessing when a child lets you into their imaginary experiences, for those experiences are closest to God. Play in imagination with your child and let them help you to return to a childlike, innocent and imaginary space. Let them teach you that anything is possible as long as you can dream it. Let the fun begin!

As adults we all too often forget to be childlike, to play, imagine, and dream. Taking a few minutes daily to imagine and dream about your own wants, goals and desires, a special time which is also the beginning of consciously experiencing the Law of Attraction. Focusing and dreaming, with a childlike sense creates the space where miracles can happen. Taking the time to sit for a few minutes a day to imagine and dream not only increases brain function, but it can also aid in manifestation.

Try meditating by taking a few breaths and focusing on the childlike feeling of imagination. Can you see yourself floating on clouds shaping them into whatever you are choosing to create? Imagine yourself at a table constructing your desires, from your higher self or with guides or angels. Being thankful for your creation, seeing completion and manifestation, helps to bring your intentions into reality. Whether you focus on love, peace, or anything in physical form, imagining yourself as the spiritual wizard, creating your wishes with a simple turn of your imaginary wand is both easy and fun!

Essential Oils, Crystals, Angels and more…

In order to increase imagination you may want to apply a small amount of the essential oil Juniper Berry on your crown chakra. Native Americans burn the berries to cleanse and purify the air. Can you see the berries "burning away" the veils of illusion so as to let your imagination come through clearly? Crystals that can enhance your imagination are purple amethyst and lavender quartz when placed near or around your crown chakra. Samandiriel is the angel of imagination. You can reach out to Samandiriel to help with visualization. When calling on Samandiriel say out loud, "Dear Samandiriel, thank you for helping me return to the realm of imagination so that I may create for the good of all."

Story

When my children were little we would go outside, lie in the grass to look at the clouds. We would take turns imagining what we could see in the big white fluffy clouds. Even if driving in the car, the boys would want to play this game we ironically named "Imagination". We would always take the time to see what the other could see, without judgement or analyzing. Not only did we all get to appreciate whatever the others imagined, we were then able to see something other than what we saw. It was a different vision, a different image, a different perspective. Even today, if we are on a long car trip and white puffy clouds are above, we play for fun. Bringing us out of the daily pressures of the physical world into the fifth dimensional space where joy, innocence, and laughter live.

I have had the pleasure of seeing my boys use their imagination in various ways. One story in particular is when my son was going on a fishing trip and he heard there was going to be a contest for who caught the most fish. Weeks before the tournament he would go to bed imaging that he would win the jackpot. Finally heading towards our boat, he asked me if I thought he would win. I replied that it was up to him. When the trip ended and all the fish were counted, my eight year old had won the jackpot! He imagined winning every night before he fell asleep and manifested his own dream into a physical reality.

Creation

Creation is the male energy of Imagination. It is the physical form of a thought, feeling, or emotion. Creation is the building block that brings spirituality into the material world. Whatever thought and or emotion are focused upon creates spiritual geometrics to form this physical world.

Creation can be conscious and unconscious depending its source. Applied focus or the Law of Attraction, brought together with feelings and emotional will result in the manifestation of that emotional focus. If Conscious Creators desire joy, they focus on joy. If an unconscious creator unconsciously focuses on emotional surrounding victimhood, then circumstances of victimhood can be created.

Because children lack earth experiences, they are in a more present state of awareness than many adults and simply create what they desire in the present moment, without judgement or analysis. What the present moment brings to children is whatever is in the present moment and they are happy with it. For example, enjoying a nature walk or communicating their need for food. They don't try to figure out why. They simply don't care to. It is the conditioned environment that tells them what to think or to explain why circumstances happen, as if it is truth. If they were not bombarded by conditioning, they would continue to simply "BE" and live life fully as unique expressions of God.

Part of our journey is to come and experience a duality dimension (for example; yes and no, up and down, action or reaction, etc.) in physical form. This offers souls an opportunity for the soul's evolution to return to *Itself* in consciousness, as a Conscious Creator. Having the Free Will to choose our experience and how to respond to experiences is part of the soul's journey back to *Itself*. When conditioning steps in, we have an opportunity through Free Will, to choose and return to *Conscious Creator*. Becoming aware and present to the joy, imagination, and excitement of life helps our children as *Conscious Creators* to manifest and bring their ideas into physical reality.

Research

A recent study discussed how entrepreneurs showed significantly different brain activity than that of non-entrepreneurs. The results were as follows:

- In the initial stage of brain activation, when people first recognized a problem, entrepreneurs were quicker to respond and were less inhibited. In contrast, the non-entrepreneurs were slower to recognize a problem. They also spent more time trying to resolve ambiguity before moving on.
- In the later stages of problem processing, the entrepreneurs thought more intensely about the

problem after they had already embraced it. The bottom line was that entrepreneurs frequently dove into a challenge without first fully analyzing it. They used their "gut" feelings to drive their actions. (Teran, 2014)

- Entrepreneurs consciously used their thoughts and feelings to drive their next creation or solution into physical form.
- A recent MIT brain study also showed that individuals with similar qualities as entrepreneurs used both side of their brains. The "entrepreneurs" in the study weren't any more likely to engage in exploration than non-entrepreneurs.
- However, when they did, they were more likely to activate both the right and left sides of their frontal cortex, while the non-entrepreneurs stuck with the left side of the brain which had to do only with logic and structured thinking.

These studies corroborate that when feelings, emotions and focus are included in our creative process, we can all bring our creations into physical form. Incorporating both sides of the brain, by using creativity, emotion and intention; we can produce our desired solutions and creations and help manifest goals in a short period of time.

Biblical Reference

You may be aware of the many miracles that Jesus performed while on earth such as turning water into wine or healing the sick. Genesis is the chapter where God created earth and Man. What is interesting about the miraculous stories is the significance of bringing the formlessness into form, resulting in a balanced complete manifestation. Formlessness is the supernatural part of creation, the thought, the imagination, the sacred idea. Form is where the actual creation takes place, the configuration of something. Fullness, an aspect of creation, is when the form and formlessness blend together to create matter. Matter is defined as "physical substance, distinct from mind and spirit." In physics that which occupies space and possesses mass, is distinct from energy. But, true creation is the result of mental, emotional and physical energy. It takes a thought, curiosity, emotion and physical matter to bring desires into this physical reality.

Jesus reminded us that we will do works greater than He, including miracles. When we consciously connect the formlessness with form, we are able to perform our own miracles. By including emotion and the childlike sense of wonder, we can attract and incorporate the supernatural energy in order to create in the light, for the highest good of all. "With God, all things are possible." (Mark 10:27) "Everything is possible for one who believes." (Mark 9:23) Hold on to the belief that you and your children can create and perform miracles, because it is so.

Parents/Caregivers

Reminding children of who they really are and the miracles they can perform is so important Guide children to remember that they are Gods, and if they have forgotten, remind them that they can change this world with their light filled heart. This is a supportive parenting style which takes courage, patience, and most important conscious awareness. It's helping them guide their way through a planet that is unconscious, and reminding them of their gifts and purpose in helping to bring humans and earth to full awareness. A special purpose as parents can be to provide and create an unconditional free environment, while the children's purpose may be to help the world with the evolution of a more conscious planet.

We are living in what is known as the Aquarian Age with a focus on "knowing" and on information. We decide if information presented to us is true or useful. If so we create from this information. Can you feel yourself being pulled away from life's dramas while pushing yourself toward becoming the Conscious Creator you are? By lightening up, by remembering a childlike sense of awe and wonder, you can manifest your true desires.

To assist in this process you may want to meditate by sitting in the feelings of both curiosity and wonder. Can you picture yourself as a carpenter shaping and building energy to manifest your desires? Can you see and feel the outcome, the fullness of the *All That Is*, you in your highest spiritual state of being, in the completion of your Sacred Creation?

Essential Oils, Crystals, Angels and more

Two essential oils used to connect with the male energy of creation and manifestations are sandalwood and ginger. Place a drop of each on your crown and base chakras. The crystal used to increase creation and manifestation is your birthstone. Your birthstone is the physical stone that is associated with your physical manifestation here on Earth. You can use that stone by holding it or wearing it to increase the energetics of creation. Calling upon Angel Ariel helps to assist in bringing your manifestations into physical form. Saying out loud, "Dear Ariel, thank you for providing me with the tools I need for that which I create for my and all's best and highest good." You can call upon the elementals of earth or wood to help shape the energetics of formlessness into form. Elementals are pure Earth and Nature beings here to help support and heal the Earth. They help to create wood, water, plants, air, fire and earth.

Story

Learning to be conscious creators takes practice becoming conscious, rather than focusing on creativity. My youngest son has always had a knack for creating things. He is aware of his past life as a wizard and uses that energy to manifest in physical form. Being involved with theater, improvisation and now music, he has spent the last few years designing what he wants to experience. He starting acting and manifested a few paid roles. When he started playing bass, he would simply focus on the songs he wanted to play on, and of course create it. He auditioned for a house band and in one year became a part of it, as well as formed his own band. In one year he has taught himself how to play four instruments and to sing. He laughs now and says, "Oh yea, look what I created!" and stays focused and light. He has taught us parents to step back and to let him design his own path.

Your children may or may not remember their past lives, and remembering is not a prerequisite for creativity. Being conscious of who they are now (Creator Gods), in the present moment, is what is most helpful to create whatever they truly desire.

Play

Play is a combination of Divine Oneness, Curiosity, Imagination, Nature and Creation. Add in a sense of childlike wonder and innocence and you have a recipe for Play. Play is uninhibited, creative, cooperative and explorative. It can be constructive or destructive, structured and/or unstructured, physical, emotional and spiritual. Because of the Universal and lighter energies, play calls forth the Plants, Animals, Elemental, Fairy, and Angelic Kingdoms to join in on the fun. Play can heal the emotional, physical and spiritual bodies. Play includes the use of all senses and chakras, removing blocks that do not serve the higher purpose. Most important, play is a state of presence. It is whimsical, imaginative and allows Source to freely flow throughout the present moment.

Play introduces children to the Universal Law of Cause and Effect. Thoughts, behaviors and actions create specific effects which manifest and create an outcome. If we are not happy with the effects or outcomes, then we must change the causes that created them. For example, if a child builds a block tower which keeps falling down, they may change how they build the tower by creating a stronger base. Or, if a child is playing baseball and wants to hit the ball to right field, they may have to change their stance.

Play also shows children the Universal Laws of Harmony, Fellowship, and Free Will. Through cause and effect they experience outcomes to be harmonious in nature, in which energies flow or stop. In the Universal Law of Fellowship children experience working with others to complete a task and/or goal using their Free Will to choose the outcome. Play provides the educational tools children need to figure out how to experience their environments, without other people "teaching" them. The Universal Laws are already set in place to help with the rearing of children. From Cause and Effect to Free Will,

Source has provided human with all the necessary tools to remember the Creator Gods we were meant to be.

Children are better without compulsory education, open to Spirit filling them up. The moment you "tell" a child what to do brings to them the thought that they are incapable. The moment you teach a child to do what you say is the moment you tell them that they are wrong. Please contemplate this. Think about all of the schools that do meditation. You know that there will be a few children who won't follow the meditation. What happens then? What does the instructor say or do to the child if they choose not to meditate?

We have to be clear that we are too close to conditioning. We are so close that even in the idea of making the world a better place, we use that to "TEACH" and to condition our children as to what we believe is right for them. (Yes, this even includes this information that I am writing to you). Can it be left up to children to be guided by their experiences, by the Spirit that freely moves through them? Can adults trust that Spirit will guide them towards their higher purpose? They have access to all the information they need. We just need to give them the space to do so.

Research

Before beginning, I highly recommend taking a look at the National Institute of Play. They can provide plenty of research in support of play in all its forms. My goal is to touch upon a few research elements in hopes of providing a better understanding of the benefits of play. (www.parentingscience.com/benefits-of-play , n.d.) According to the National Institute of Play:

- Play is essential for the growth and maintenance of brain cells.
- Play improves memory and stimulates the growth of the cerebral cortex.

- Play improves attention after children have had a recess--an unstructured break in which children are free to play without direction from adults.
- Pretend play increases both receptive and expressive language.
- Play contributes to the ability to solve divergent problems. An example of a divergent problem is attention and the ability to reason.
- Pretend play correlates with the ability to self-regulate.
- Preschoolers who played with blocks had better math grades and took more math courses as teenagers, than those whose play time did not include block games.
- Children as young as three understand and make distinctions between realistic and fanciful pretending. They use information learned from

realistic pretend scenarios to understand the real world.

Biblical Reference

Zachariah 8:5 states, "And the streets of the city shall be full of boys and girls playing in its streets." The reference is about how Jerusalem will be the city of the second coming of Christ. I'm not asking you to think about the second coming of Christ, but rather to contemplate the Christed energy, especially the Christ Consciousness within. Christ Consciousness feels similar to being a child playing, celebrating, laughing and being present to the moment. When we take the time to quiet our minds, we become like children, allowing consciousness to guide us.

Jesus also said, "Let the children come to me; do not hinder them, for to such belongs the kingdom of God. Truly, I say to you, whoever does not receive the kingdom of God like a child shall not enter it." "He took them in His arms and blessed them, laying his hands on them." (Mark 10:13-16.) Jesus never disciplined a child. He welcomed their innocence and their playful acts. He calls upon humans to follow His lead in order to enter into the kingdom of Heaven. He encourages us to become like children, to be playful, innocent and be open to receiving all that heaven provides, for that is how to create heaven on Earth.

Parents/Caregivers

Please sit with your children and play. You may want to play outside, roll in the grass, toss a ball, play a board game, play video games, draw, make forts, dance, make music and sing. As adults we sometimes get so caught up in being a parent that we forget to be playful. You can take a moment to stop, using the time your child is playing as an opportunity for you to become playful and to connect with them. You can play with your child while being present to the Christ consciousness within you. Please accept the invitations into their world, observing what they want to share with a kind heart, being grateful for the opportunity.

Most unconscious adults are woken up by alarm clocks, go to work, come home, eat dinner and repeat, forgetting to create opportunities for play. We've become so conditioned to living the American dream that the cost has been giving up the joy of life for surviving. Learning to bring play back into our lives can sometimes feel like another chore but trust me, its value and worth is unsurpassed. Play's energetics can heal the physical body, assist with daily problem solving, and can clear blockages within the emotional body. Play can make us laugh, create confidence and it simply makes us lighter.

When meditating, learning to play with the energies helps to experience what we have always known. Being playful during meditation adds curiosity and joy to help us remember who we really are. It brings us deeper into a state of awareness, feeling light and full of energy.

Essential Oils, Crystals, Angels and more

The essential oils that can help bring back more play are Frankincense, Lemon, and Peppermint. You can add a drop of each to the solar plexus. The crystals that can aide in being more playful are lemon quartz, coral, and moonstone and can be placed in your pocket or near the solar plexus area. When calling on the elementals, you can choose according to the type of play. For example, if you are at the beach, you may call upon the water elementals. If playing outside, you might call upon the earth and wind elementals. When asking the fairies for help with play, you can build tiny fairy homes in your garden or near trees to thank them for their assistance. To bring more fun and joy in your life, try praying to Angel Jophiel saying out loud, "Dear Angel Jophiel, thank you for bringing fun back into my life and for creating balance within my mind, body, and spirit."

Story

I asked my husband what his favorite memory was when playing with our sons. He said his favorite was when we would get together with his family in the mountains. We'd rent a cabin, eat a lot of yummy food, and play games. There were no computers, no video games, just a lot of laughter.

Every year our boys pack bags full of Nerf toys to add to the fun. They pick teams and run up and down the stairs, chasing each other. It is a never ending weekend of laughter, giggles, and strategy.

I asked my husband why that memory stood out above the rest. His response was, "It makes me feel like a kid again."

Nature

Nature is defined as the collective physical world. It is Mother Nature encompassing plants, animals and landscape. Nature provides nourishment and sustenance, protection and replenishment. Nature is in a constant state of change and is creation in its perfect form. The movement of the oceans, the change of the seasons and the cycles of living things demonstrates how the flow of energy can be smooth and at ease or destructive and chaotic.

Children embrace the changes in Nature constantly by adapting to its ever changing cycles. They build snowmen during winter and swim in the oceans, lakes and rivers in the summer and jump in piles of fallen leaves in autumn. Children fill their souls with the energies Nature provides. They walk barefoot in the grass grounding these energies. They climb trees for strength, smell flowers for clarity and jump in rain puddles for pure joy. They easily connect to the plants, trees and animals in the space of unconditional love. Mother Nature is so giving while children know exactly how to enjoy her.

Research

One of the greatest teachers of Nature is Richard Louv who wrote *The Nature Principle*. He covers extensive scientific evidence in the support of spending time outdoors. Below is a short list of Louv's findings:

- Spending time in nature increases a human's ability to scent track as much as other animals.
- Individuals who spend most of their time outdoors have increased abilities in sight, sound and ability to detect danger, as well as being able to view whole surroundings, compared to those who spend most of their time indoors.
- When in nature humans have the opportunity for optimum learning, using all the senses at the same time.

- Direct contact with nature can help with mental fatigue, restoring attention, and helping the brain to process information.
- Nature can calm the mind.
- Nature can increase memory performance and attention by 20 percent after only an hour.
- Nature can increase academic achievement, problem solving skills, motivation and the ability to learn new tasks.
- Nature can increase creativity and independence.
- Nature can increase neuron function, help with pain control, stress and provide an overall better outlook on life.
- Nature can boost the immune system, improve self-esteem, and provide a feeling of well-being.

You might enjoy *The Nature Principle* by Richard Louv for more information and research on Nature.

Biblical Reference

The Bible states, "But ask the animals, and they will teach you, or the birds in the sky, and they will tell you, or speak to the earth, and it will teach you, or let the fish in the sea inform you. Which of all these does not know that the hand of the LORD has done this? In His hand are the life of every creature and the breath of all mankind." (Job 12:7-10) The Earth was created to support Man in all his glory and wonder, as the "perfect image of God." One of the greatest gifts given to humans was the gift of Mother Earth herself. She is the nurturer and healer, who loves and gives to us unconditionally. She offers knowledge and wisdom to children through her natural examples of the Universal Laws of Nature, without force or judgement.

Parents/Caregivers

Spending time with children in nature can transform families. Not only does Nature provide everything needed for the physical body to survive, it also provides the emotional and spiritual requirements needed to move Earth and its habitants into full Conscious Awareness. You and your children are a part of the transition taking place. By embracing the gifts the Earth has provided, whether spending time outside daily, growing gardens and/or connecting with the Elementals, children are better able to understand their purpose. As children connect with their True Nature, their True Source, they replace the chaotic with peace, clam and well-being. The calmer, centered feelings we experience, the more the Earth will return to her higher order. One way to experience more calm is to connect with our own personal Earth Star which is located below our feet in the Earth.

Essential Oils, Crystals, Angels, and more

We are spending a lot of time indoors. The essential oils of sage, sandalwood, and Siberian pine nut, can help to bring Earth energies indoors. Placing a few drops on the soles of the feet can help to increase the energy and connect to Mother Earth. The crystals which increase the energetics through the Earth Star are obsidian, smoky quartz, and turquoise. Placing them in your pockets or near your feet can provide increased energetics. All of the Elementals can be called upon when in Nature, depending on where you are or what you are doing. For example, if at the beach calling upon the water and earth Elementals can help to provide opportunities for health and well-being. Calling upon the loving energy of Mother Earth and her creations can help you to connect to your Earth Star, saying out loud, "Dear Mother Earth, thank you for helping me to create opportunities to connect, ground, and heal myself, through my Earth Star."

Story

We have always enjoyed being an outdoor family. While camping, hiking, and gardening, we have loved embracing the gifts Mother Earth has offered. I remember that at the end of one summer we were returning home from a trip in the mountains and stopped to have lunch and to enjoy the forest before heading back to the city. We pulled the camper onto a dirt road, set up some chairs and ate lunch. As we sat and enjoyed the weather, a large butterfly kept circling around the boys. The more relaxed the boys became, the more the butterfly would circle and land on them!

I remember a similar situation. I'd driven my sons to the zoo to pet the stingrays. I mentioned to my eldest son to tap into the stingray's energy. Once he did, he reached his hand out and the stingrays swam up to him, letting him pet them. Other children would reach out, but the stingrays would only dive underwater and swim away.

I have always encouraged my children to play, explore, and to connect with Nature. Because of that they have been able to experience a deeper connection with the beauty and serenity which Earth is offering us.

Grace

Grace is the benevolent gift of ease, and/or assistance from the Divine. It is also a state of awareness where Pure Source resides in Love and Compassion. Grace is the gentle, unspoken love and mercy delivered by the Holy Spirit. It is the moment when a child reaches for your hand, grabs an apple from a tree to eat, or raises their face to the sun. Grace arrives when they fall, finding solace in a comforting hug or in gratitude for the keys to the car. It is the unexpected helping hand when options have run out, a holy moment, transcending both time and space.

Research

Grace is akin to gentle kindness.
- When receiving or witnessing acts of kindness, the chemical oxytocin is produced in the body which can aid in lowering blood pressure and improve overall heart-health. Oxytocin can increase self-

esteem and optimism, which is helpful when anxious or when we might feel shy.

- Individuals reported that they felt stronger and more energetic after providing service to others, feeling calmer and less depressed, with increased feelings of self-worth.
- People who were gracefully generous with finances felt overall happier.
- According to *Love and the Brain*, giving help to others protects overall health twice as much as aspirin protects against heart disease. People who gracefully volunteer for two or more organizations have a 44% lower likelihood of dying early.
- Moments of grace can stimulate the production of serotonin. This chemical heals wounds, creates calmness, and makes us feel happy.

Biblical Reference

In Acts 20:32, Jesus reminds his disciples the power of God's grace by saying, "And now I commend you to God and to the word of his grace, which is able to build you up and to give you the inheritance among all those who are sanctified." Through God's grace anything is possible. Through God's love, the kingdom of Heaven awaits you. When we are aware of the presence of Source, whether through us or a child, we enter the kingdom of Heaven through the experience of present moment. When we are conscious to Source that lives in all of us, we are able to move past the conditioned habits and allow the holy experience to be guided by love, joy and compassion.

Remember, we are created in the perfect image of God and are able to experience His grace in every moment. That is what creating heaven on Earth is.

Parents/Caregivers

Being present to the everyday Grace around our children has the power to melt mountain tops and calm any storm. Seeing and feeling God's Grace around and through every sacred moment opens the door for more grace to enter. It takes awareness of the present moment which is filled with unconditional love, mercy, and sometimes forgiveness to appreciate grace. Being present in the moment where Grace may step in can "make your day!" Grace comes in both wonderful and challenging times, allowing love and mercy to flow through any situation even when not requested.

Grace is not always something we are taught or shown. Having to go through many personal losses and tragedies, I seemed to push the idea of Grace further and further away. However, taking the time to become aware of the little moments of Grace creates more Grace. The gentle love of waking in the morning is now an opportunity to be thankful for Grace, which is the recognition of the Holy Spirit embracing us.

When meditating, you can focus on both your crown chakra located on the top of your head, and the sacred heart which is behind the physical heart. You can feel the gifts of the Holy Spirit moving through and providing you with God's Grace, Love and Mercy. Can you feel the loving presence, a golden white light coming from the crow chakra down into the sacred heart, flowing through and around you? This is God's Grace.

Essential Oils, Crystals, Angels, and more

The essential oils used to attract in Grace are Edelweiss, Easter lily and Rosehips. You can place a few small drops on the physical heart. Placing Jasper and Hematite on the physical heart as a necklace can be used to assist with Grace are Jasper and Hematite.

Calling upon the elementals of light, water and air can help to whisper signs of Grace to you throughout your day. Finally, praying to the Holy Spirit can help you become more aware of the many gifts of Grace. Saying aloud, "Dear Holy Spirit, thank you for showing me the gifts of Grace, Love, and Mercy bestowed upon me throughout my day. Please show me how to be Graceful."

Story

I have experienced many moments of Grace with my sons from holding them as infants to the healing of an illness. One day my youngest son and his two friends went to the park to play. As children sometimes do, two (including my son) of the boys teased the other and the young man's feelings were hurt. When we got home, it dawned upon my son that he had made a mistake by hurting his friend's feelings. I remember standing in the kitchen and asked my son if he wanted some advice. He agreed. I made a suggestion to call his friend and apologize for his actions. No one answered. My son hung up the phone looked at me and started to cry. Truthfully, in that moment a part of me wanted to say, "I told you so." But, in what I believe was a moment of grace; I stopped and just held my crying son. In his moment of grief something made me pause and to be present. He did not need someone to scold him. He already knew his mistakes and simply needed someone to comfort him in his time of need, without any judgements. This was a moment of Grace for him and for me.

Gifted Education, Special Education and Alternatives

Gifted education highlights students who have been tested who are capable of performing above average within an educational setting. There are those students who can perform above average, but there are those who may never take the test or score low who are gifted in some other fashion. There are students who are gifted in art, music, dance, and sports that will never see or spend time within a "gifted" classroom. If we look at the research on creativity and the research by Rosenthal on teacher perception, it is understandable that students who are raised in a gifted class or environment, believe themselves to be so, therefore ending up furthering their pursuits supported by academia. However, what I have seen and experienced from children raised without compulsory education, similar outcomes occur. These students end up pursuing their own interests and excel beyond their "school" aged peers. They are able to take risks and deal constructively with failure. Self-directed learners view learning as an adventure, rather than experiencing "burn out". They become life-long learners and pursue those degrees that support their interests and passions.

Special education is different. Children who are born with special needs have committed to come into this world not only in part for their spiritual evolution, but to show those who love them their gifts and talents in a unique way. As parents and teachers, it is our responsibility to be open to learning and listening to them utilizing more than the physical world. Many students are adept at telepathic communication and require telepathy to help them navigate in this world. Letting them take the reins to guide us to the next moment can be life changing for them and for us.

One great parent's story is from a friend whose son was diagnosed Deaf and Autistic. The mother felt in her heart that her son came into this world to teach her a different way of being. Every day her son came home from school and would go outside into the backyard and look down their backyard fence. His mom became "curious" and wanted to see what he was looking at. She followed him outside. After he was finished with eyeing the fence, she did the same. What she saw was amazing. She said she had never seen the fence from that perspective and found it exhilarating.

Taking his lead to understand from his perspective, gave her a small understanding of why he liked to view the fence that way. He gave her a different perspective which she most likely would have never seen before. This brings me to the idea that instead of seeing "special children" as less than or incapable of performing academics, it would be more beneficial to see them as truly special, capable of showing us their gifts and talents in a special way. They provide insights of how learning happens differently.

These students often require more assistance than regular students. Think of it, similar to a stroke patient who can no longer stand or talk. However, through therapy they can achieve much of what was lost. Some of our students require therapies to help them through their daily struggles. But, if their therapy is causing them to struggle more, or they are finding school boring or laborious, seeking out different therapies which can reach these students in a different way could be rewarding for them.

One of my clients has a daughter who struggles with walking and with expressive speech. The walking did not bother the child but she would get upset when her parents did not understand her. The school system wanted the child to receive both physical therapy and speech therapy. The daughter did not want to go to physical therapy so the mother only scheduled speech therapy. To this day, the daughter is as happy as can be and is able to communicate with her parents without difficulty. The daughter knows she can go to physical therapy whenever she is ready, without coercion.

My son went to occupational therapy for three years. His therapist played games with him which helped him tremendously with the sensory issues that bothered him on a daily basis. One way she helped was by desensitizing him when he was exposed to loud noises. Being in tune with students, their needs and frustrations is vital to knowing how to help them best. It is most valuable to learn to ask these special children for guidance (if they can speak) what they require or what they want to learn.

Living in the United States allows parents the opportunity to homeschool. Some states have requirements while others do not. Self-directed learning on the other hand may include homeschooling, some schooling or none at all. Having the child pick their pursuits to learn as they grow allows them to trust in themselves and gives them the courage to try new things and to take risks. Other educational alternatives can be beneficial in that they sometimes utilize curriculum and assessments. However, they are under the belief that the child must be taught something in order to learn.

In Sugatra Mitra's Hole in the Wall study, he showed that children were capable of learning whatever they want without the help of a teacher. The closest option of self-directed learning within a school is Democratic schooling. Students in these schools have the freedom to organize their daily activities, utilizing democratic decision making. Students can go to lessons if they want to or can play outside. They create the rules and follow their interests and pursuits, without manipulation, coercion and or grading.

It is understandable that not everyone can go to a Democratic school or can be homeschooled due to their current circumstances. Even though your child may attend a public compulsory school, it is how you respond to things that can make a world of difference. If they get a bad grade, are bullied, or seem to not be enjoying school, responding to those situations in loving discerning, nonjudgmental way will help you and your child come up with solutions you never thought possible. It may mean changing classrooms or schools, to ensure your child's safety, happiness and well-being. Breaking the conditioning of compulsory education and its daily effects on you and your child is sometimes a challenge. However, allowing love into the process greatly ensures that a solution will soon be on its way.

Essential Oils, Crystals, Angels, and more

Hyssop is an essential oil that can be used to support caregivers and parents. Placing a small drop of Hyssop on the solar plexus promotes balance, inner peace and calm, forgiveness and faith. Most of all it is incredibly helpful in connecting with the love and guidance of Angels. Placing Red Amethyst on the solar plexus can bring energy of courage, tenacity and inner strength. Finally, praying to Arch Angel Michael can help to provide you with strength and support. You can say out loud, "Dear Michael, thank you for your unwavering support and guidance. Please provide me with the spiritual strength for the best and highest good of all."

Mary's Message

Dearest Ones,

This is Mother Mary. I have come to share with you from the Highest Light, spiritual understanding, truth and a message of Hope for the children of your Earth realm. Before I begin, I would like to discuss with you one of My many apparitions.

The moment I visited three young children in Fatima, Portugal, I came to them not only because of their faith in myself and God, but because they set an example for others within your physical realm of how children of the Earth hold one of the many secrets to bringing your dimension into full consciousness. I entrusted my message to them because of my awareness of their innocence and their lack of developed egos. The children on your planet incarnated with the knowing and state of consciousness closest to Source. It is when they become surrounded by the conditioning of your physical environment that the barrier of separation, of remembering who they really are and their capabilities, clouds their existence.

When I appeared to the three children, I wanted to show those and you that when a child is given trust and knowledge they can perform miraculous events, they can help transform your planet into a higher state of consciousness. When children are free to express and experience naturally through the Universal Laws God has provided them with, conditioning will fall away and Christ Consciousness will exist more fully.

I ask you Dear Ones not to only observe the Presence of every child unconditionally, but most important to observe yourself so as to not impose your own thoughts and behaviors onto them. The more you become your own higher state of consciousness the better the children will be able to examine their own existence on your planet without the handicap of a conditioned mind.

I ask of you to please take care of the children on your planet, especially those who are at the hands of war for they are the most vulnerable to conditioned environments of manipulation and control. These children are in need of love and play. They need to be rescued from the violence they have and are witnessing. They need time to heal from their physical and emotional experiences. I ask that you do whatever is in your power to ensure that these children are embraced with unconditional love. It is through their emotional and spiritual healing that ideologies will fall away so that Christ Consciousness prevails. For once they see and receive unconditional love, and have their physical needs met, they will remember who they are and will ensure that future generations do not experience the monstrosities they have endured.

Support your children in their passions and interests and trust their guidance. Do not judge their experiences and allow them to form and create their own lives always believing that they are the Creator Gods they were meant to be. Listen to your children and help them when needed. Embrace the moments spent with them for within them is truly the Kingdom of Heaven, filled with joy, laughter, and innocence. Pray for your children and those on Earth. Give up your worries to God and the Angels for We are listening and watching over children in every sacred moment.

I thank you for this experience. Feel my presence around your home and in each present moment. Call upon me when you need me and I will be with you providing love and comfort to you and your families. Love and guide your children without conditions and or judgement and you will open the doors to experience endless miracles. And with that I say, Amen.

Conclusion

Parents struggle everyday wondering what to do next or how can they help their children. From my own experiences, I logically knew that concerns about reading, writing and math came secondary to what may have been physically wrong with my children. If we went to bed and awoke in the morning alive and well, then that is all that really mattered. All we want as parents is to have our children be safe, healthy and happy. Deep down we know this is true yet our conditioned thoughts about school and the need for it hinder us from focusing on daily functional skills needed for survival. Luckily there are tools that can help us get beyond the repetitive thoughts. Below is a list of individuals and tools that have helped me and my family along this journey of self-directed learning.

Mastering Alchemy with Jim Self

Jim Self is more than just a mentor, he is a friend. Before I started with Mastering Alchemy, I already knew how to meditate and did so to quiet my mind. I searched for someone to show me how to be more conscious in the present moment or during times of struggle. Meditation has been transformational for me. However, Jim's tools provide me the ability to notice my thoughts and consciously create what I desire for myself and my family. He offers a free Level 1 introductory course at www.masteringalchemy.com.

Eckhart Tolle

Eckhart's books *Power of the Now* and *A New Earth* are two of the many books which helped me to become more aware in the present moment. Eckhart's teachings showed that suffering comes from thoughts rather than being aware in the present moment. Eckhart offers many online classes and seminars to further the practice of "being in the now." They are available at https://www.eckharttolle.com/.

Anastasia and the Ringing Cedars Series

Looking to create and build a Space of Love for you and your family? If so, I highly recommend the Ringing Cedars Series books written by Vladimir Megre. The original series was written in Russian about a Siberian woman named Anastasia. Anastasia is a surviving member of an ancient Vedic civilization whose has extraordinary powers and knowledge can change the world. These books are about a "new dawn" unfolding and an "eco-village revolution" taking place. These books can be found at https://www.ringingcedars.com/

The Medical Medium with Anthony Williams

I heard about Anthony Williams recently as I was seeking health alternatives for myself. When I came across his book I was so impressed with the medical knowledge he wrote about, especially for someone who did not have a medical background. "Anthony has a unique ability to converse with a high-level spirit who provides him with extraordinarily accurate health information that is often far ahead of its time." I highly recommend his book *The Medical Medium*. His information has helped my family tremendously and we will be forever grateful. His website is http://www.medicalmedium.com/.

Creative Outcomes

If you are looking for an educational organization that supports parents who choose alternative learning, you may enjoy *Creative Outcomes*. This group not only offers extensive research, books and resources on alternative education, but they also provide support, training and guidance to parents learning to raise children through self-

directed education. They can be found at
http://creativeoutcomes.org/

James Titschler, I AM Oils

I met James by taking one of his Chakra Harmony meditation classes in town. I was so impressed with the effects of both the meditation and essential oils that he created that I feel I need to share. In fact, it was after the first meditation that I was able to focus and produce my first draft of this book. James is definitely on to something that can help those who battle the daily conditioned habits that keep us from being who we really are. He can be found at http://www.theempowermentpath.com/

Lorna Byrne, Author and Speaker

I have read Lorna's books and love her authenticity. Lorna has seen angels since she was a baby with as much clarity as we see people. She offers information on how to connect to your angels as well as shows us how angels present themselves to children. She is an activist for children suffering in war torn areas and continues to support her local communities and families with messages of hope. You can find her at http://lornabyrne.com/

Martha DuSage, Author, Speaker, and Healer

Martha speaks out on abuse of both adults and children. She teaches how to integrate the heart with all parts of self that bringing about truth, light and beauty to the darkness that resides within us all, thereby allowing all parts and all voices of self to harmonize. She can be found at http://marthadusage.com/

Elizabeth Welles, Actress, Author, Speaker and Healer

Want to create more creativity? Looking to find your voice through art and writing? Elizabeth is an "artist with the tools of healing, dedicated to nurturing the seeds of creativity, joy, and peace that reside in the human heart." She tells stories in a variety of venues, from NY to LA, on stage, in television, film and radio. You can find her at http://elizabethwelles.com/

Most important, you may simply want to listen to your gut feelings. If something does not feel right or if you feel that school or advice seems like a constant battle, you can take a step back and possibly begin to ask questions, seeking out research and support. Finding balance between what others think is right and what really works in your situation can only come from you. I always try to breathe and focus in on the feelings of "neutral". That seems to put me in the space where there is no thought, no worry of what's to come or how things are.

Remember there is no right or wrong and *it's not your fault.* Conditioning goes back for generations and the point that you are trying to stay in the present moment takes courage and strength. The only requirements your children have are food, water, shelter and unconditional love. Putting those before anything else ensures your child to create a self-sustaining, secure future, not only for them but for future generations to come.

Personally I have witnessed these Universal Laws of Learning through my own children and friends alike. I am not perfect by any means but continue daily work on my own conditioning and fears. Every day brings new experiences and just like you, I try to walk the spiritual path as best as I can. Even if it means two steps forward and one step back, I ask my children for forgiveness when I screw up and hope there are no scars left behind.

I am so grateful for all who have taken the time to read this book and I am excited about the potential and possibilities for more families to find joy and fulfillment.

I encourage parents to form local support groups. Learning to become aware of our own conditioning and allow our children to create their destinies takes practice. Learning to listen to our own Higher Selves and to trust Spirit to guide our children goes beyond rational thinking. Having the support of like-minded individuals helps us to get through the three dimensional chaos to bring us back to who we really are. Every day I practice on becoming a consciously aware parent. It is not always easy but with the support of my friends, I am able to move through my personal struggles and be there when my children need me.

Know that your child picked you as a Creator God, as their earthly parent to help in the awareness of conditional habits in learning and education. They picked you to smooth the path in order for learning to be truly conscious, fun, and driven by Spirit. By using the Universal Laws of Learning, together we can create change and allow children the gift to design their own learning through curiosity, interest, and their own spiritual guidance.

May God bless you and your families and may He provide you the strength and courage to allow and discover the beauty of the *Universal Laws of Learning*.

Appendix A: Bibliography

Divine Oneness

Nierenberg, C. (2016, May 20). The Science of Intuition: How to Measure 'Hunches' and 'Gut Feelings'. Retrieved August 02, 2017, from https://www.livescience.com/54825-scientists-measure-intuition.htm

The Pygmalion Effect. (1968). Retrieved August 04, 2017, from http://www.duq.edu/about/centers-and-institutes/center-for-teaching-excellence/teaching-and-learning/pygmalion

Isaiah 59:1-2 *(New Revised Standard Version)*

Curiosity

What Does Dopamine Do? 26 Surprising Dopamine Effects (18 are good, 8 are bad). (2017, June 23). Retrieved August 02, 2017, from https://selfhacked.com/blog/dopamine/

Davis, A. F. (2014, October 06). Curiosity helps learning and memory. Retrieved August 02, 2017, from https://www.universityofcalifornia.edu/news/curiosity-helps-learning-and-memory

John 4:48 *(New Revised Standard Version)*

Mathew 18:3 *(New Revised Standard Version)*

Imagination

Ferro, S. (2013, September 16). How Imagination Works. Retrieved August 04, 2017, from http://www.popsci.com/science/article/2013-09/how-imagination-works

The importance of imagination in children's development. (2015, November 26). Retrieved August 04, 2017, from http://www.1stplace.uk.com/the-importance-of-imagination-and-creativity-in-childrens-development/

Sir Ken Robinson on the Relationship Between Imagination, Creativity, and Innovation. (n.d.). Retrieved August 04, 2017, from http://www.conversationagent.com/2015/08/imagination-creativity-innovation.html

Can Creativity be Taught? Results from research studies. (2017, June 30). Retrieved August 04, 2017, from http://www.creativityatwork.com/2012/03/23/can-creativity-be-taught/

Genesis 1:27 *(New Revised Standard Version)*

John 14:12 *(New Revised Standard Version)*

Creation

Terán, P. T. (2014, August 07). Entrepreneurs' Brains are Wired Differently. Retrieved August 05, 2017, from https://hbr.org/2013/12/entrepreneurs-brains-are-wired-differently

Kamenetz, A. (2014, September 24). MIT Brain Scans Show That Entrepreneurs Really Do Think Different. Retrieved August 05, 2017, from https://www.fastcompany.com/3004746/mit-brain-scans-show-entrepreneurs-really-do-think-different

Mark 10:27 *(New Revised Standard Version)*

Mark 9:23 *(New Revised Standard Version)*

Play

National Institute of Play: The cognitive benefits of play: Effects on the learning brain. (n.d.). Retrieved August 06, 2017, from http://www.parentingscience.com/benefits-of-play.html

Zachariah 8:5 *(New Revised Standard Version)*

Mark 10:13-16 *(New Revised Standard Version)*

Nature

Louv, R. (2011). *The nature principle: human restoration and the end of nature-deficit disorder.* Chapel Hill (N.C.): Algonquin Books of Chapel Hill

Job 12:7-10 *(New Revised Standard Version)*

Grace

Did You Know? (n.d.). Retrieved August 07, 2017, from https://www.randomactsofkindness.org/the-science-of-kindness

Love and the Brain. (n.d.). Retrieved August 07, 2017, from http://neuro.hms.harvard.edu/harvard-mahoney-neuroscience-institute/brain-newsletter/and-brain-series/love-and-brain

Acts 20:32 *(New Revised Standard Version)*

Acknowledgements

Thank you to my sons and my supportive loving husband. This book would not exist without you. You are my biggest teachers and show me every day how the Universal Laws of Learning work. You are three of the most conscious creators this planet has ever seen and I enjoy creating more planetary adventures along with you. Thank you for choosing me as your mother and wife! Because of our experiences and spiritual journey together, the evolution of consciousness on this planet has shifted.

Thank you to Martha, Chrissy, Gayle, Zhena, Colleen, Elizabeth, Vanessa, Tatanya, Rachel, Peggy and Judy, my soul family and friends who have consistently encouraged me to complete this book and put it out into the world. You have all helped me fulfill this purpose for today's youth. Because of this experience together, and because of your encouragement, love and support, children of the world have hope to live in a planet of their own conscious creation.

Thank you to so many others, especially to my family and friends, who are willing to connect to Source, in order to play, imagine, listen and simply allow our children to create the lives they are meant to live.

About Tracy

Tracy Brooker is often introduced as a teacher, a healer, an educational intuitive. She has led educational seminars and has professionally taught special education for almost twenty five years. After her first son was born, she started a business as an educational consultant, guiding teachers and parents. As an entrepreneur and mother, she has successfully built an educational coaching business while supporting the passions and interests of her two boys.

Since childhood, Tracy has felt that she would become a teacher. Consciously, even as a young girl, she was able to work with energy, learning to follow her intuition to create the life she always desired for herself and her family. For years she has incorporated various modalities of spiritual energy tools and techniques such as Reiki. Tracy delights in guiding professionals and families to develop their Consciousness.

Combining her knowledge and love of both education and spirituality, she has written *Universal Laws of Learning* and has cofounded *Creative Outcomes*, a nonprofit business supporting the philosophy of Self-directed Learning. Furthermore she has designed the *Conscious Education Academy,* a web series helping families to *consciously* co-create Peace and Well-being with themselves, at home, at work, in the learning environment, and throughout the planet.

www.tracybrooker.com